Emancipation Rivers

Also by Anthony B. Ashe

Relationship Related and Other Poetry

Emancipation Rivers

Anthony B. Ashe

Reconstruction Books Publishing
Mitchellville, Maryland

Reconstruction Books Publishing
Mitchellville, Maryland

www.reconstructionbooks.com

Cover photograph courtesy of the Anthony B. Ashe archives

Cover design by 1106 Design

Printed in the United States of America

printing number
1 2 3 4 5 6 7 8 9 10

ISBN-13: 978-0-9789752-2-7

Library of Congress Control Number: 2007930653

To Anthony, Aaron, Abraheem,
and Austin for saving my life.

Table of Contents

I

Was it Bo Bo or Boon Deen who died?   11

Checking out   15

Scriptural   19

Mask Asleep   23

II

April Fools' Day, 2008   27

New York Historical Society: Postcards from
Photos of Lynchings   29

Breathing   33

On which track does the next train stop?   35

III

Emancipation Rivers   41

MYANMAR: Cyclone aftermath photo   43

China   45

Sestina redux   49

IV

YOUR BED IS NOT MY BED 55

Aubade? 59

The Gnosis of Late Sunday Mornings 63

Toes and hips 67

THEY WERE FIRST 69

V

Sestets 73

Couplets 75

Rap and refrain 77

A Son Came Forth 81

Grandpaspective 83

Epidermis 85

Excerpt from the soon to be released "The Autobiography of Snooky Lenox"

"Footie" 91

I

Was it Bo Bo or Boon Deen who died?

Harlem sings abroad
Harlem's sung in tongues
Harlem blue tears dry,
watching Bo Bo and Boon Deen fly

Harlem buses, bulged with bumpers
(Boys held on for life and rides)
Minds too bruised to re-collect
whether Bo Bo or Boon Deen passed by

Harlem, mourning on its corners,
Blinking through the eyes that lived
Harlem's holding back its tears
'cause it's got no more to give

Harlem streets under Harlem feats
paving layers running red
Harlem grief through gritted teeth
Was it Bo Bo or Boon Deen who was dead?

Harlem hears with Harlem ears
Listening through a deafening hush
Kids run fast 'cause moms beat ass
with lullaby hands,
pinning washboarded clothes
to laundry lines
strung over tenement garbage
in backyards
as backdrops

for
Ringalieveo dodging cars —
Was that Bo Bo or Boon Deen's crushed
head?

Harlem's ever cloudy rumors
never yielding to the light

Fresh Harlem faces
sing Harlem's praises,
was it them passing by?

or

Constructive memory
gentrification?
recalling Bo Bo or Boon Deen's expiry sigh?

Visitors tell the Harlem news
offering romantic views
cleaning up the Harlem air
rescuing from what was there

Harlem aches, then Harlem cries
as circling Harlem pigeons fly
Harlem shows off Harlem things
like Sunday bells that clarify
with answers about which brother died —

Checking out

The funeral parlor awning:
"WHERE BEAUTY SOOTHES YOUR GRIEF"
A grey whiskered mouth
on Lenox Avenue yawning
at a
fledgling mother
in too deep
extracting
a blackhead
reflected
in the silver public phone —
cleavage bulging
from an exhausted blouse,
burnt pomade
straightening comb
adherence,
acrid latrine
costumed
as the
side of a
red/brown
stone dwelling —
four billboard Mojitos,
a fifth being poured
over
pimp/heroes
protecting crack

prostitutes'
minty cool
pastels
won't be ignored
women
indemnified against
John abuse —
dusty oxidized steeple
standing agape,
envious
of copper eyes
and
acute olfactory.

Scriptural

The resolution in the repetition of
"Amen" and "I know thass right"
confirmed the preference
of platitudes over the profound

The aisle to my left,
on the other side of glazed eyes in nodding
heads,
mocked me for the walk I'd never take
or taken

I fought with sleep during biblical references
irrelevant to the sound-bite sermon,
then awoke to the heels of the female minister,
who I only lusted after in my heart,
scuffing their way past me during the
recessional hymn

Prayer/part one:
"I promise to live well, God, if you extend my
life"
"I promise to be faithful, God, if you send me a
wife"
"I promise philanthropy, God, when you're
saving various children from starvation and
strife"
"I promise to pay attention, God, when you
offer insight."

Prayer/part two:
"Please send me a nightlight that stays on in
the day,
to ease my fear of sudden darkness when I'm
awake,
but that can be dimmed when the glare is too
harsh."

Mask Asleep

mask asleep,
aortic rupture
of a heart too young
to have beat in rapture

mask asleep
through alarms
awakening
to life removal

mask asleep,
eyes closed
to polished recollections
during ceremonial tribute

mask asleep,
boxed and lowered

mask asleep,
blue-black in Carolina clay
while Mourners dry tears
with cornbread sopped in collard green juice.

II

April Fools' Day, 2008

The Spruce Pines
lining Interstate 85
in Anderson County
shadow South Carolina troopers —
in daily shined shoes and
taut Sam Browne Belts —
hunting twenty year old Niggericans:
corn rowed, tattooed, and college educated —
in violation
only
of laws
requiring enough facial hair
for shaving.

New York Historical Society: Postcards from Photos of Lynchings

remnants hang still from bare branches
stripped and butchered
cold in detached dignity

residing where
spirits from captured images dance
in release

tattooed backs turned to deaf audiences
escape
while weaving fibers into textiles
on Nat Turner's loom

shackled epiphany
whispering from Great Dismal Swamp
gasping from surrender
to a january emancipation heard in june

when reconstruction faked freedmen out and
into the saddle
where buffaloed soldiers rode high
and swung chariot low
as manifest destiny tools
"comin' for to carry" themselves "home"
from San Juan Hill and Belleau Wood
where malodorous recollections
of charred oklahoma and florida screams

witness a neck stretching to skin threads
because texas pickups don't slow down
to stop at trees

cocked heads bask in refracted light
through formaldehyde jars
on shelves displaying emasculation trophies
in view of the promised land

then "citizens,"
browsing for mules,
are shadowed down forty-acre aisles
as though shoplifting their own stores

Breathing

Beret wearing
Bud Powell,
Richard Wright
under nauseating Eiffel Tower/Statue of Liberty
altitude —
French kissing
Napoleon's tomb,
Rodin's sculpture, and
electrical outlet adaptors —
unmolested on the Tuileries
by staccatto "Excuse me can I help you sir"
translated into:
"Get the fuck out of Bloomingdale's please."

On which track does the next train stop?

this
individual
intrusion —
asking broken
tourist questions
uninhibited
by
a dredlocked fence

innocent —
of
bordered lore
concerning
underclass proclivity
and pierced
ears

unconcerned —
re: the
dilligence
of crossing a street
in
acquiesence
to
hackneyed fears —

aware
and
in agreement
that
visibility
should
be seen,
with
condescension
desirous
of pardon

INVISIBLY annoyed,
by this subversion —
clothed in shiny, whiskey hued pleather
(the kind that a newly minted cab driver likely
wore
when inheriting correct enunciation of the "n"
-igger word,
finding that it satisfyingly followed the f – – k/U
word
when slowing without stopping
for four hundred years of ancestry
painted into a twelve hundred dollar suit
hailing a ride
in order to ensure arrival
at the ballet
on time) —

responses dealt themselves
(though surprised by recognition and
acceptance of the event)
without celebratory note
or
stereotypical incident

Emancipation Rivers

Like lavender Dogwood
painted on a fading Nottaway County canvas

or green fruit
fallen from miscegenated ancestry trees

and liberty juices
gulped by babies born loose of bondage into
unsquelched tears

passes and passers
as ironic keys
to civilized doors

invigorating
freedom side chill
on emancipation rivers

dreams and dreamers realized
chattle minds in promised lands

left and lost are sacrificed
breath on breadth of calloused hands

manumission override
lists on ships are left behind.

MYANMAR: *Cyclone aftermath photo*

Pause
inhale
taste
rancid death air
sustaining frailties

waiting for water,
Babies search with furtive eyes,
in ill-fitting clothes

tear-salted
chewed
lip
hunger pang
abatement

One Girl and Two Boys,
vacuous faith and black pail,
all with close-cropped hair

old
man
shiny-star
epaulet ornaments
sleep in dry beds.

China

my cups are chipped
and
the saucers
were either
left in the Salvation Army Thrift Shop dish
section
or
discarded by the dowager
who rewarded my grandmother
with hollowware
when she retired from feeding her family
on inflamed knees
then stood up
to display callouses
as deterrents
for acceptance of gifts
in the future

my cups
have no answers
for:
"plate is to table as . . ."
standardized test questions

my cups
are stained brown
with residue
from re-re-used teabags

my cups amazed
then embarassed me
with the discovery,
on their bottoms,
of my geographic ignorance
— angry, I closeted them
unaccompanied
by
blue
bamboo
and pagodas
glazed
on
matching bowls
and plates

Sestina redux

Light reigning
down
through
cumulus blue,
in mourning
for dancing children.

Children
stand under skies, raining
morning
down
in blue
notes, merely passing through

threw
glowing children
into asphyxiation blue,
strangled by hands reigning
with trickled down
neglect and mourning.

When morning
returned to dusk through
sundown,
children
sang in the raining
night to tunes that winds blew.

Whispers blew
kisses to mourning
survivors reining
in tears that threw
children,
holding them down.

Kept down
by black eyes and blue.
But children,
resilient, wake with the morning.
Thriving through
the reining.

Children celebrate through
blue mourning
raining down on their dance.

IV

YOUR BED IS NOT MY BED

I am crisp
in creased October, open-windowed sheets

I snooze my alarms
before finally gathering for pushups and prayer

Then, empty bladder
and measure coffee in silence

In your bed you breathe
soft in and exhalation
through sculpted lips

Mine now empty
is not your bed

My sheets now inanimate
without your curves

Curtains give way in willing submission
to chilled gusts absent of your scent

Day breaks
onto knots in my wood floor
swirling without your footprint

Intent on
a cooing, lingering bird
I search for your voice in its insistence

You stir,
in half sleep in your bed

I cannot feel the weight and warmth of your
turning

Aubade?

Three alarms on three clocks,
his allergies don't arrest him
when he wakes in the dark

She wants nothing louder
than her circadian rhythm
and has already forgotten
the volume of her voice
as she repeated his name
into the candles

He remembers stirring once
on Grand Cayman at noon
squinting and reaching
for his black Ray Bans.
The Sun will not surprise him again

She covers her head
with the sheet and quilt.
The bracelet
that she was too aroused to remove
snags in her disheveled hair

He stares east unblinking
out of the bedroom
light should be brimming now.
Moving silently west
to the living room view
he watches for reflection

She slaps at the snooze
on the one she can reach
from her side

He smiles and returns
when the rusty hues
mirror those from his crew cut
in old photos taken
before he was seven

Her foot cramps.
She curses his compulsion
blaming him for the spasm

He moves back easily
into the indentation
in the soft mattress
that he left cooling

The sky blinks
then peeks
with its focusing eyes
through a slit in the curtains

She softens
then yields
to accept his return.

The Gnosis of Late Sunday Mornings

in bed with orange muffins,
two sugar/one milk coffees —
brown next to burning legs draped
in magnetic skin —
lingering semen, cavity juices,
and sweat
flaring nostrils —
The New York Times Magazine Crossword
Puzzle.
Here,
where caprice avoids collision.

We,
of documented IQs,
skimmed
from "The Talented Tenth,"
armed
with "Post Traumatic Slave Syndrome,"
the knife
for psyche incisions
and
intoxicant in
castigation addiction
or
deafening echo,
less intrusive than the silence
of

cumulus filtering
of
blinding glare.

We,
metaphor tenor,
deliberately absent a vehicle —
association so apparent,
the reader of us is assaulted
by enlightenment.

We,
symbolism,
beacon on visual literacy.
That,
and pungent new-cut grass.

Toes and hips

swim in sheets with
breasts to lips.

Is this two tongues or one as
we silhouette against whatever light there is
left burning in the candles and
struggling through the shades?

Is 2 am
illuminating the distance
between the drawer that you emptied for me
and
the underwear still in my apartment?

Is the heat that we generate inadequate
for the soothing
of muscles aching
from our exercises
in futility?

and . . .

Why is the absence
of the pads of your fingers,
tracing the skin covering my spine,
so readily apparent
when I'm alone doing laundry?

THEY WERE FIRST

or
    he was
then
    she,
    rib
    from ribs —
    not like barbeque,
    but
    still
    salty/sweet,
    on the tongue —
one
    from near his heart,
    imprinted
    with his
    pulse

her top
    two front teeth:
    slightly
    seductively
    gapped,
    insignificant
    before
    The Bite

V

Sestets

fitted hats crowning glory
reigning,
bleeding embryonic conciousness
from Huey Newton, Bobby Seale veins
mad at madness
exercising futility

poisoned soil crippling sown seeds
sprouting feral defiant weeds
aimless race on mangled limbs
humming worn out battle hymns
hypocrite truths self-evident
reconstruction lost lament

on tattooed arms and psyche scarred
the soul on tap through threatened bars
the challenge of day into days
and angst of navigating ways
of grasping to remain alive
the how abandoning the why

impending coming precious young
singing songs as yet unsung
by sons of fathers yet unborn
threatening promise yet untorn
undaunted by life's lofty lies
dare through fearless, hungry eyes

Couplets

from darkness bared and soul on soul
on ice and reason to be cold

the whys and what they signify
the how to be excuses why

from blackness cleansed and soul the goal
on ice and listing in the cold

the clear, and thus, the magnified,
the how to be, the justified

in shrouded darkness soul is sold
to highest bids from stories told

the thoughts and lettered answers cry
to heave disheartened endless sighs

in light of blackness soul unfolds
how hope through darkness still takes hold

in words and reason clarified
that birth is certain just to die

Rap and refrain

fitted hats crowning glory
reigning,
bleeding embryonic conciousness
from Huey Newton, Bobby Seale veins
mad at madness
exercising futility

from darkness bared and soul on soul
on ice and reason to be cold

the whys and what they signify
the how to be excuses time

poisoned soil crippling sown seeds
sprouting feral defiant weeds
aimless race on mangled limbs
humming worn out battle hymns
hypocrite truths self-evident
reconstruction lost lament

from blackness cleansed and soul the goal
bent now from listing in the cold

the clear, and thus, the magnified,
the how to be, the justified

on tattooed arms and psyche scarred
the soul on tap through threatened bars
the challenge of day into days
and angst of navigating ways
of grasping to remain alive
the how abandoning the why

in shrouded darkness soul is sold
to highest bids from stories told

the thoughts and lettered answers cry
to heave disheartened endless sighs

impending coming precious young
singing songs as yet unsung
by sons of fathers yet unborn
threatening promise yet untorn
undaunted by life's lofty lies
dare through fearless, hungry eyes

in light of blackness soul unfolds
how hope through darkness still takes hold

in words and reason clarified
that birth is certain just to die

A first boy baby
is the sun for the father,
a dawn paternal

A Son Came Forth

Seed to root to bud to bloom
A chest grows full and has the room
for light to beam like full sunned moon
A son came forth and far is soon

The trees then stretched to reach up high
to call and capture heaven's eye
A son came forth and cleared the sky
To rest on wings with strength to fly

A breath of clarity at last
A son came forth with die uncast
By gleaming eyes and questions asked
Paternal face is life unmasked

The son came forth to reap his own
The fruit, the ripened, fully grown
The harvest gathered from the sown
The son, a father fully known

Grandpaspective

Fast,
like two- and three-year-old eyes and feet
and
the hummingbird that they missed.

As fast as
time between asleep and awake
and
racing hearts thumping against miniature rib
cages in
anticipation of frozen Kool Aid or
crayons and construction paper.

Fast,
like "I'm hungry" and "I have to pee"
or
as fast as
"how to hold a baseball bat" directions are
discarded.

Fast,
like small hands with big hugs or
new smiles dry old tears.

Fast,
like snapshots yellow,
like limber becomes arthritic,
like grandsons are grandpas.

Epidermis

The Bible,
on the lamp-lit bed table;

The Art of War
on the peeling
and rusting TV tray's
snowy scene —
crammed additionally
with extra bifocals,
short wave radio,
Webster's blue and red plastic
New World Pocket Dictionary,
and translucent urinal.

The gold
Pullman Porter pocket watch
in it's velvet-lined box
(already bequeathed to his eldest son,
who will bequeath it to his eldest son)
and the flipping numbers
in an illuminated clock-radio
on the sill
of a ground-level window
are inventions
of diminishing significance.

The most recent sponge bath
(ritually administered
by his day nurse)
is put to use
as visitor entertainment;
there is too much
of who he is
that can't be consumed,
so he's squeezing out of himself.
Readily, his evacuation
of housing that has become inadequate
commences.

Excerpt from the soon to be released
"The Autobiography of Snooky Lenox"

"Footie"

I

I was twelve and in the sixth grade when I first heard another boy say Footie's name:

"Some fourteen year-old kid named 'Footie' beat up Spade; Can you believe it?"

"Damn," I answered, suppressing a grin, "That's a shame. Didn't Spade kick your father's ass last week?"

"That ain't funny, niggah. He took that shit out on me for two days after that."

"All I'm saying is, that kinda means that a fourteen-year-old whipped your daddy's behind."

"Fuck that. Any way … supposedly Spade was slappin' some woman around—Footie wasn't havin' it and put that motherfucker in the hospital."

"Damn!"

A few days after that, I was working up the nerve to try to buy a bottle of Wild Irish Rose when I heard some grown-ups talking about him as they came out of the liquor store on Convent Avenue and 129th Street.

"Somebody said some boy beat some drug dealer half to death last week 'cause he was hurtin' some woman over some money."

"Damn. Who was it?"

"Don't really know. Somebody said his daddy is that karate school guy up on 136th and Amsterdam."

II

The belfry at Church of the Master echoed eleven times—the number that I counted in my head as I shook my loose fist, feeling the black-spotted white dice bounce against my palm.

The bells inside of Adam Clayton Powell Junior High School would also be ringing, signaling what should have been the change in periods for me, from French to Earth Science.

I was a winner behind the red brick, public toilet building in the park on 123rd and Morningside when two other teenagers, both bigger and older than me, began arguing over whose turn it was to roll next.

Immediately after the crack of hand on cheek, I heard a baritone exclaim, "I came out here to make some money, CUT THAT SHIT OUT!"

Turning toward it before "OUT," My own lips pursed to spit "who the fuck …", and were met by twin irises that were indistinguishable from pupils, and barely a shade darker than the shiny skin on a broad face that almost yawned in nonchalance. The knuckles on both of his hands were healing. I choked on the rest of my sentence as the dice settled, showing a three and a four on top.

"Whassup Footie?" One of the former combatants mewed, then "sorry, sorry" and "everything's cool" to each other and the voice.

III

Two weeks before the end of the school year, I was arrested and suspended for punching Mr. Booker, the science teacher, in the neck when he yelled at me for not removing my books from my desk during a quiz. After he fell into the classroom doorway, I stepped over him and went out to the teachers' parking lot where I deflated his tires with an ice pick, then exploded his windshield with a chunk of broken sidewalk.

The chair near the window in The Nation of Islam Barbershop across the street offered an unimpeded view of Mr. Jones's reaction when he stepped out of the school and moved toward his car.

"How would you like it, young brother?", the bow-tied barber asked.

"Short on the top—fade the back and the sides."

I wanted to be a "Black Muslim." I hadn't yet read *The Autobiography of Malcolm X* and didn't know that he had split with "The Nation" before his murder. I didn't even know that he'd changed his name, so after having my neck cleaned with hot shaving cream scraped away by a straight razor, and witnessing the teacher lifting his trembling hands to cover his tear-streaked face, I went next door to "Steak-n-Take" for a steak with cheese on whole wheat and a copy of "Muhammad Speaks."

That summer I was sent away for two months to Camp Woodside in North Middleton, Connecticut, somewhere near where, it was rumored by "campers," the owner of "McDonald's" lived. We were all from New York, Boston, or some other Northeastern city, and the density of what we saw as a forest surrounding Camp Woodside eliminated the necessity of a fence. There was a swimming pool, and we slept in tepees, covered wagons, or hogans. We played "Capture the Flag" and had "backwards" days when we wore our clothes with the labels in the front and ate meat loaf for breakfast. We had a canteen that sold potato chips, cupcakes, and soda, and we were able to collect mail and care packages there. Aunt Tiny (my grandfather's eldest sister) began sending me the tins of oatmeal chocolate chip cookies that I later came to appreciate when I went away to college.

I finally cracked my "ice grill" into a smile when my mother wrote that my six year old brother had been questioning her about when I was coming home.

"Oh yeah," she wrote on one occasion (or maybe it was just "P.S."):

> Puppy came by and asked me to tell you that some boy named 'Footsie,' or something, was shot and killed in the school park on 124th and Morningside the other night. Why can't those boys use their real names? I'm sick of having to remember all of these nicknames that don't make any sense. I better not have anybody coming up to me referring to my son "So and So" by some name I that didn't give you. I will not be claiming you if that ever happens. Anyway, try to have some fun and be a good boy.

"Footie," I said aloud. A "counselor" was near enough to hear me. I must have made a subconscious decision to have this death notice appear more significant to me than it was, because the pale lanky orangehead, whose name I couldn't remember, because there were so many smiling white overseers there, looked at me like I think that I must have looked at

Buster, my dog, when he was the scrounging, bony puppy that I found in the rain.

"Terry," he said, extending his right hand. "What's happenin' dude? Is everything okay?"

"My mother just wrote to me that a friend of mine was killed."

The look on his face invited tears to brim in my eyes, and I accepted my role in the unfolding drama when Terry began to recite his lines:

"Why would your mom write to you about something so horrible?"

"She only knew his real name," I lied, "Somebody told her about it and used his nickname."

"Don't worry. We're all here for you and I'm sure your group-mates will be supportive."

The evening before my mother's letter, I'd crawled under the tarp covering the tepee that housed the fourteen year old girls, and slid next to Dorothy, who was from The Bronx, in order to continue the tongue-kissing lessons that she initiated on the path to the pool just before lunch. Her eyes remained closed but she opened her mouth to me immediately. Only when I began to unbutton her pajama top did she show resistance.

"Stop," she whispered, "Somebody's gonna hear us."

"C'mon, I only want to touch your titties a little bit."

"Stop I said!" then she pushed me to the floor where I stayed in order to slither back out of the same gap that I'd come in through.

During the night, after receiving the letter, Dorothy startled me with her sudden warmth in my bunk in the covered wagon. "I feel so bad for you and your friend." She kissed me before I was fully awake and unbuttoned her own top in order to place my hand below her breast and on her heart.

The air was thick with sweaty socks, sleepy farts, and the perfume that wafted from under Dorothy's nightshirt. She lifted it and straddled me, only to let it drop as she lowered her hot gripping wetness onto my erection. I remained quietly in a dream until she shifted her hips and my shuddering body forced a feral grunt from my lips.

I fell soundly asleep and she was gone when the wagon crew, T.J., Weasel, and Headache, woke me at sunrise for us to take our scheduled turn making breakfast.

We flipped pancakes and opened jugs of real maple syrup (a revelation to me after 14 years of Aunt Jemima).

Throughout the rest of the day, people tilted their heads and gave me little solicitous smiles.

"Are you okay?"

"Do you need something from the canteen?"

"You shouldn't hold your feelings inside."

"How did 'Footie' get his name?" asked Elizabeth, a short, thick-ankled blond girl from New Haven with a seductively nasal accent that I'd never heard before, had concern etched on her face to an extent that I couldn't have matched, even if Footie had been my best friend.

"He wore size twelve shoes when he was in the fifth grade," I answered.

"It was that, at first, then it became because he was quick to put his foot in the ass of anybody who fucked with him." I expected Elizabeth to recoil with the inclusion of the last bit of information. When she didn't, I felt an immediate, inexplicable affection for her.

Elizabeth waited with her face open to me and I was confused about what she expected. With an aching stomach, I began to think out loud about Footie:

> His real name was Emanuel. He was a little shorter than me, but his body was more built, more muscular-like. He was about two years older than me, maybe.
>
> I never heard about him being afraid to fight, but I know that sometimes he stopped them. Girls always wanted to be around him, but he had a girlfriend, Sunny, who he really liked. She ain't all that pretty, but I seen her make him smile.
>
> His father is some kind of a karate sensei I think, and his mom might be a teacher's aide or something.

I began to miss my own mother and remembered how rarely her freckled cheeks rose to reveal her gapped-tooth smile after her father died.

I didn't know much about death, but I knew that I couldn't eat the peanut butter and jelly sandwiches with cherry Kool Aid that the girls from the tepee had prepared for lunch.